Sam

Baseball Boys

Bumblebee Books
London

BUMBLEBEE PAPERBACK EDITION

Copyright © Sam 2021

The right of Sam to be identified as author of
this work has been asserted in accordance with sections 77 and 78 of the
Copyright, Designs and Patents Act 1988.

All Rights Reserved

No reproduction, copy or transmission of this publication
may be made without written permission.
No paragraph of this publication may be reproduced,
copied or transmitted save with the written permission of the publisher, or in
accordance with the provisions
of the Copyright Act 1956 (as amended).

Any person who commits any unauthorised act in relation to
this publication may be liable to criminal
prosecution and civil claims for damage.

A CIP catalogue record for this title is
available from the British Library.

ISBN: 978-1-83934-059-8

Bumblebee Books is an imprint of
Olympia Publishers.

First Published in 2021

Bumblebee Books
Tallis House
2 Tallis Street
London
EC4Y 0AB

Printed in Great Britain

www.olympiapublishers.com

Dedication

To my Lord and Saviour in Whom I am not worthy of.

Chapter One
Jack and Jake

Greetings, I am Jack, and I am one of a set of identical twins. My brother is Jake. We like to play baseball, or at least I do. Jake, on the other hand, loves baseball. He lives, breathes, and always thinks about baseball. I only play baseball because Jake does. I'd rather do a science experiment or analyse the roots of a tree. As you can see, I am what people call a nerd, but I don't mind. This is who I am.

Ever since we were four years old, we played baseball. Jake is amazing when it comes to that ball in his hand. I, on the other hand, am not as good. But, I don't really care. I'd rather have him in the spotlight than I.

There is something about having an identical twin. Yes, we both have brown hair, brown eyes, light-coloured skin, and we are the same height and weight. Everything about our appearances is exactly the same! So, you cannot tell him that he's ugly, because you are basically telling yourself ugly. But that is not what baffles me. What baffles me is how EVERYBODY mistakes me for Jake or vice versa. Yes, we clearly look the same and sometimes we dress the same, but our personalities are completely different. Jake is a fun, loving jock who attracts everyone to himself. Clearly, he is some so-called people magnet. I am a rather calm, collective scientist, or should I say, nerd. I cannot attract people to me to save my life. Jake says it's because I am too much of a 'fun sponge,'—like that is a word, whatever he means.

I will forever remember this day in the year of 1998. As usual, my team got ready to play. The catcher was Frances, or by her nickname, Frankie. She was an overweight tomboy with brown hair and blue eyes. She was also my brother's crush. I don't know how, nor do I know why he likes this peculiar girl, but he does. The pitcher is, of course, my brother, Jake. Since he is the best on the team, he has the #1 on his jersey. On first base is my brother's best friend, Randal, or by his nickname, Randy. He is a tall Mexican boy with a personality similar to my brother's.

On second base is Daphne, or by her nickname, Daffy. She is a goofball with black wavy hair and dark green eyes. She is so beautiful! Not that I like to say it, but she's my crush. Short stop is Lincoln, or by his nickname, Lin. He is a proud jock and I do not particularly like him. Third base is a short Pilipino boy by the name of Jamael, or by his nickname, Jay. He's a singer. He literally sings EVERYTHING; even if he's talking to us, he'll answer us in a song. Out in right field is me. In the middle field is my best friend, Geoffrey, or by his nickname, Geo. He is a short black boy who admires science as much as I do, but the love of baseball that he owns is much like my brother's. In left field is

Sandra, but we call her Doll, for sometimes she only pays attention to her looks, rather than the ball. She always has a lollipop in her mouth.

Then there is Saul, an autistic kid who likes to hug people. We call him 'Hug Man.' He is also Lin's younger brother. I feel bad for Saul. I would NOT like to be Lin's brother. The usual back-up catcher is a kid who goes by the name of Snickers. We don't know his real name, only that he LOVES Snickers bars. The last good player on the team is a girl by the name of Rose. She is a happy, hopeless romantic kind of girl. No lie, she put lace all over her uniform. Then there's the other Frances. We call him 'Weird Frankie' because that's the ONLY word that describes him. He eats his own boogers which is completely weird and unsanitary!

As I was saying, I will forever remember this day. As our team, the Stars, got ready for the Bears to come up to bat, I got a funny feeling about this day. It was a sickening feeling. I cannot describe it, but I had a feeling that something horrible was going to happen.

The first Bear came up to plate and my brother wound up his arm. Strike one. The Bear as I can see from the outfield looks nervous. He has probably heard that my brother can submarine pitch and throw a pitch so hard it reaches 100 miles per hour. And it is very true. Strike two. Then the last pitch was a fast left-handed pitch. Strike three. Oh, I forgot to tell you; Jake can also throw left-handed and right-handed.

The next Bear came to the plate. He was not nervous at all, which may have been a big mistake. Jake gave him a fast ball at 100 miles per hour. That certainly jawed him around, for he is now shaking with nervousness. Then the next one was fouled off. Then strike two. The next one was a hit straight to Daffy. She caught it and threw it to first. Thrown out.

I saw from the distance, Jake growing pale. He has been passing out lately, which has been very baffling to me. But, he has only passed out after a game, NEVER during a game. So, when he grew white, I wanted to stop the game and sit him down. But, sad to say, I didn't. First strike. Second strike. As he wound up for his famous right-handed submarine pitch, he fell to the ground, unconscious.

I screamed out his name, hoping that my brother would awaken. But he didn't. I ran to him as an ambulance came to take him away. I shook him violently as tears streamed down onto my brother's face. A stretcher came and took away my twin. I tried to get in with him, but they wouldn't allow it. I didn't realise it then, but my brother was not unconscious, but in a never awaking slumber. They needed to revive him. I was paralysed as the ambulance ran toward the hospital. They were taking him away.

My mother grabbed me and led me by the hand as if I was six years old to our car, while my fourteen-year old sister, Destiny, and my twelve-year old brother, Jefferson, followed us. My mother started the van and started to speed down the highway to the hospital. As she sped, she tried to comfort us. I didn't hear much of what she said except, "… Dad… come… hospital… Jake… okay." But, will Jake be okay? I am so scared that he will not be okay. My life as I knew it, though I did not it realise then, was going to change from that day forth.

Chapter Two
You Never Thought That It Would Happen to You

We went into the hospital and I remember my mother asking where Jake's room was. The nurse at the desk told her that it was on the third level and that only one person at a time may see him. One person at a time? I could tell that that meant no good. I know, I sound ludicrous when I am horrified. We went up to the third floor and found Jake's room. I allowed my mother to see him first, but from what I heard from the receptionist was that he wanted me. So, my mother told me to see him.

I never thought I would be so afraid to see Jake, until then. I was shaking all over my body. I was so nauseated that I remember tasting vomit in my mouth. I slowly walked in the door. I saw him and he looked as if he was dead, but I knew he was still breathing. An air machine pumped air into his lungs. Other machines and pumps connected to him, some I do not know the name of. I never thought a boy of sixteen would be like this. An eighty or ninety-year-old man, or maybe sixty, but never sixteen! He was healthy, fit, and active. How he came to this horrific fate baffles me to this day.

I came close to him and he, as he is, brightened up at my presence. He reached out his hand and grabbed mine. He then laughed at his own situation, as I knew he would. But, I was in no laughing mood.

"Jake, why are you laughing?" I asked seriously.

"Don't you see the humour in it?" he replied.

"No, this is serious. They won't allow your own mother in here if there is someone else visiting you."

"But, don't you see? I was up for the pitch and then bam! I hit the ground."

"That isn't funny. Jake, stop laughing. You might hurt yourself."

"No I won't! I was making the EMT's laugh the whole way here! Well, except for when I was out. C'mon, don't be a fun sponge!"

"Jake, just settle down for a little. Will ya, for my sake?"

"Okay, for your sake, but really, lighten up."

"I will, when the right time comes—" and he interrupted me by mimicking me in a weird voice, as he always does.

You know, most people act seriously in the hospital because it's a serious place. But, not Jake. No, he will never grow up, even if he's old and on his death bed. Jake will never grow up, a 'Peter Pan' as I call him when he's good to me.

"Jake, stop that!" I cried, frustrated.

"Okay," he said with a sudden weakness in his voice, "I'll stop."

What? No protest? Now THAT is not the Jake I know. I know for certain something is wrong with him. "Are you okay?" I asked, concerned.

"Yeah, just suddenly tired," he replied. "I don't know why. Hey, can ya send Mom in here?"

"Uh, sure, no problem. Get well—" and I left him, wishing I could say more.

Then I sent Mom in. Once she was gone, I started pacing the waiting room. I was nervous and that was not a good thing to show towards my younger siblings. Soon, my little sister started crying. I didn't know what to do. Usually Jake was the comforter. I was never good with people skills, even with my younger siblings. I sat beside my sister and as Jake did, I laid her head on my chest, though it was extremely uncomfortable. I tried to comfort her with all the comforting words I knew, but that did not do any good. In matter of fact, it made it worse. That was when Jefferson pushed me away and rebuked me for troubling her. I didn't understand what I did wrong. So, I left her and the waiting room.

I soon found myself in the kitchen? No, that is not that word. It was a sort of cafeteria room. I went to the vending machine and bought myself a Dr Pepper and a Snickers. I sat at a table and found myself staring at the nutrition facts on the Snickers bar. I never knew how unhealthy candy is!

I heard a voice behind me. It is a very familiar voice. I turned around and found my father.

"Father! Oh, Father!" I cried and threw my arms around him. I would never admit this to my friends, but I let myself cry upon my father's chest.

He pat me on the back, knowing what I'm going through. My father was always an understanding man. I cannot remember one instance in my life that my father did not understand me. He was much like me and Jake combined: a scientist and yet, a people person.

"I know son. I know," he said.

"Father, have you seen him yet?" I asked.

"No, Jefferson told me of the way you ran out of the waiting room."

"Oh, Father, do you think he's..." I couldn't say that word. I don't think anybody can truly say that word when it has struck you or one that you love.

"I don't know, Jack. C'mon, let's go back to the waiting room."

"I can't just sit down and wait for the diagnosis!"

"There's nothing that we can do, but wait."

So, I reluctantly followed my father back into the waiting room. My little sister was no longer crying and Jefferson must be with Jake, for my mother was in there. Soon, everybody went and saw Jake, but no results.

After everybody saw him, they started running more tests. EKG, MRI, X-ray, blood tests, brain scan, etc. Never in my life have I heard of a boy needing so many tests, nor have I seen Jake that scared before. They let two people in the room when he was taking tests like having his blood drawn. Father knew I wanted to stay with Jake, so he let me, though he wanted to be in there himself. He also knew that Jake wanted me there to comfort him. I couldn't comfort him with words, but as I saw in his eyes, just my presence sufficed him. Mom also was in there. I should have let my father be in the room at the moment, but I thank God for letting me be there for him.

I will never, no not ever, forget when he got a spinal tape. You see, they didn't know what was wrong with him, so they did all kinds of tests. I will never forget his scream as they pushed a huge needle into his back and swerved it around. And his eyes that expressed such fear and pain will never leave my memory. I can still hear it and see those eyes to this day.

It was eight at night when they were done testing him. They haven't got a diagnosis, nor the slightest clue of what is the matter with my brother. I can see it in their eyes. I can see their fear. They are not very good actors. My father insisted for me and my mother to stay with Jake, since there was only one car and they boosted his visitors to two people at a time. So, my father left Mother and I at the hospital.

Once they were gone, my brother called for me. "Yes?" I replied.

He grabbed my hand and squeezed it, for pain shot throughout his body, especially his head.

Tears well up my eyes as I said, "If I could take away your pain and put it upon myself, I would do it in a heartbeat."

He looked up at me and replied, "I know you would and I would do the same for you. Jack, I don't think I can play baseball anymore. Could you…"

"No!" I shouted. "Of course, you can play. You'll be out in no time!"

"No, I won't. On that ambulance, I died. They had to

revive me."

I pulled away from him, shaking my head as I shouted no.

"Yes, I did. Look, you need to be the captain of the team. I can't do it anymore. Coach ain't much help and I can't take…"

"No, you're going to be better!"

"I'm not! You need to pull your weight on the team."

I looked away from him and hid my face, so that I could cry.

"Jack, come here."

I reluctantly came to him. I got onto my knees and laid my head upon his bosom. I grasped his night gown and wept. I found little comfort from my childish actions.

"Look, Jack, baseball's my life and without it: who am I?"

"You're my brother! You can play baseball!"

"No, I can't. Please, Jack, do this for me. Until I get better, will you be the Stars' captain? Will you be brave for me?"

I looked into his eyes and I saw a great need, no, a desperate need, for me. I was so afraid to take up this great task. I don't even know one thing about leadership. That was Jake. I am a follower. With all of these cons, I still nodded my head yes to his desperate plea.

But, if I cannot take away his pain, who can? I would give away my life for his pain to be taken away. I did not know it then, but my question was to soon be fulfilled.

Chapter Three
The Diagnosis

It was ten in the morning when I woke up in a hard chair. I don't remember getting up and going in the chair, but I am regretting ever sleeping in that chair. You know, for a hospital, they have chairs that can give you a disease, such as scoliosis. I seriously think I will be in the hospital after that horrible slumber!

Well, I got up and found Jake eating lunch? Is that a sandwich? Wait, it can't be lunch! It's ten!

"Hey bro!" Jake cried. "You know it's twelve? You slept like a little baby; Mom didn't dare wake you up."

"I wish she did," I said, rubbing my neck. "Dang, did that chair hurt! I'll be in the hospital next to you if I sleep in that chair again!"

Jake laughed. I love his laughter. I am not much on describing things that are not science, but here I go. His laughter was like a thousand angels singing a chorus in tune. He was a song that I can still hear over and over again. It became my so-called forever theme.

"I'm glad you're laughing," I cried. "Don't I always?" he replied.

I smiled and grabbed his hand. "You know brother, we will be missing school today."

"That's the bonus of being sick: no school!"

"That's the problem: I love school."

"I know you do, nerd."

"And I love being one, jock."

"And I do too!" he laughed.

"Knock, knock!" cried the doctor and he came in. "How's my patient?"

"Better, Daddy-o!" cried Jake like the complete goof he is.

I rolled my eyes. Jake will forever be my goofy twin. My better half.

"Well, keep that happiness in mind because," the doctor droned on, "I have some bad news. I don't know how to say this…"

"Give it to me straight!" Jake demanded and he squeezed my hand harder. Seriously, I'm gonna end up here after him because of that chair and my brother's strength.

"Well, Mr. Davidson, you have a stage four cancerous brain tumour that wraps around your whole entire brain. That's why you have been passing out. And the reason for you needing to be revived is because that cancer has reached your heart. If you do not take chemo therapy and you will see, at the most, three weeks. Or you can take chemo therapy and you will see, at the most, three months."

"He has cancer?" I choked.

"Yes, he does."

"And he's going to…?"

"Yes, unless a miracle happens, but the likely of that is one to a thousand."

I couldn't bear it. That room was surrounding me like prison walls and I was chained up to those walls. I needed out of that room now! Tears streamed out of my eyes as I ran out of the room and out of the hospital. I didn't know where I was going, just somewhere away from my worst fear granted. So, I took the bus and went across town to the place that belonged to my brother, the baseball field.

Chapter Four
Taking Over the Team

I looked around and sad to say, I think I went crazy. I saw my brother, not as he is but as he was. He was playing baseball like he always did. He was throwing a fast pitch. Now, I hear him calling out my name. What is he saying? Snack trout? I cannot differentiate the words coming out of his mouth. He shouts again. I ask him what he means, but I get the same Charlie-Brown-adult answer. Then everything went black.

I woke up to a face. A very familiar face. Once my mind stopped scrambling, I perceived it to be Frankie.

"Hey, you okay?" Frankie asked, concerned.

"Didn't you hear me yell?" Randy asked.

"Why moping?" asked Hug Man.

"Hey, you're crazy for doing that!" Lin shouted.

"I'm here for you," Geo cried.

They all spoke at the same time; it hurt my head worse! I couldn't bear this shouting at me, so I yelled for them to be quiet. They stopped at this sudden outburst, for I was usually quiet.

I got up from off that horrible bench! I am serious,

all these horrible resting places will ruin my back! I grabbed my back and groaned.

"Are you okay?" Geo finally asked.

Tears came into my eyes, tears of sadness and bitter anger. None of them has ever seen me cry, except for Geo, of course. I didn't know what to do, but to stuff my eyes with knuckles. And let my tears flow.

"What's the matter?" Geo asked and scooched close beside me. The rest of them just stared.

I looked at them all and said, "Jake is no longer the captain, nor will he ever be again. He has stage four cancer and he has three months. I'm the captain now."

"Oh Jake!" Frankie mourned and cried into Hug Man's arms. "This can't be!" Randy sobbed and banged up his bat angrily.

"Randy stop!" shouted Geo and everybody stopped crying. "Look, Jake may be dying, but we need to get him something that he always wanted, the national championship trophy. And we cannot get it if we mourn his death when it is not even here! Yeah, we all know that Jack isn't the best player, but he was picked by Jake. And that means a lot. So, let's get out there and practice! Anyone with me?"

"Why should we listen to HIM?" asked Lin.

"Because," I got up, "My brother is the one who was elected captain and HE was the one who trusted me with this position. If you don't want to be part of this team or make my brother proud, then you can leave."

Lin looked at me, bewildered. Then he replied, "For Jake, you will be my captain."

"That means you will need this," said Frankie, and she gave me Jake's whistle that he kept there. I put it over my head and shouted, "Let's go out there!"

We lined up in our usual places and then I realised something; there was no pitcher! So, I decided to make it different. So, I put Saul in my place and I took Jake's, for now. I was pitching, but I was not good at it, at all. I kept going over Frankie's head, or on her side, or too low. I am definitely not a pitcher!

Finally, I decided to do batting drills for the rest of the day with the pitching machine. After practice, my father came to the field.

"There you are!" he shouted. "I've been looking all over town for you! C'mon, we need to get Jake's room prepared for his machines. And look at your pants! You ruined your pants! Let's go."

So, I got in the van and we drove home.

Chapter Five
The Next Morning

I woke up at the sight of a bright light. I had had a horrible nightmare: my brother got put in the hospital and he had stage four cancer. I was sweating all over and my body was shaking. I needed to prove to myself that this was just a dream. I got up and went into Jake's room. No one was in there, just a room full of baseball and hospital equipment. Then I realised this wasn't a dream, but a reality. A horrible, frightening, nightmare-like reality.

I heard my name and I, emotionless, walked downstairs. There was only my parents in the dining room. I found a pile of pancakes at my seat, but I didn't want to eat. There was a horrible knot in my stomach that really hurt. I just picked at my food, pretending to eat my pancakes.

"Hey honey, I know you're upset about Jake, but you need to eat. Could you just eat one pancake for me?" cried my mother.

"Yeah, sure," I mumbled. So, I ate one pancake, but it didn't taste like a pancake. It tasted something like a mixture of dung, dirt, and butter. It tasted awful!

"Am I going to school today?" I asked once I was done eating.

"No, we called the school and they said it's okay to have another day off," replied my father.

"May I go to my room?"

"No, you are coming with us to get your brother."

"What about getting dressed?"

"Go, get dressed and get your brother some clothes. Then meet us in the van."

I slowly walked upstairs and got dressed. I was never too big on appearance, unless I have a date (like I would ever have one of those). And since I didn't care about it either, I dressed in a pair of sweat pants, my colourful pair of suspenders, my t-shirt that said 'Blah!' in big red letters, and I plopped my favourite baseball cap on that said 'Science' in blue letters. Oh, and just for fun, I put my favourite gel pens in my shirt pocket.

Then I grabbed my brother's favourite clothes: a pair of blue jeans with holes in it, a green athletic shirt, and his favourite baseball cap that he signed himself, because he hopes to become famous some day and he said it would be worth millions by then. I looked at that hat, and tears welled up my eyes. He will never be what he wanted to be, a famous baseball player like his idol, Scott Bailes.

A honk came from outside, telling me to hurry up. I ran downstairs and locked our house door. I came into the van to silent parents. It was odd, for my mother never really stopped talking, but not for my father. He may be a people person, but he's just not talkative when things are so serious.

I sat there and thought. Being a natural thinker and

worrier, I thought horrible thoughts. Thoughts that are too horrible to mention, well, at least for me. You probably not think the mentioning of death and pain is not too horrible, but it is for me.

We were soon at the hospital and in my brother's room. As I came into the room, a smile appeared on my brother's face. It was so beautiful!

"Hey nerd! I see that you're wearing your favourite cap," Jake cried.

"Hey jock. Yeah, I didn't feel like brushing my hair. How are you?" I replied.

"Better, because I get to go home today!"

"I got your clothes, so you don't have to wear your baseball uniform."

"Thanks buddy, but I gotta wait until the nurse — there's the cutie now! You came to help me change?"

"Your brother can do that," she replied, "but I came to take you off the machines for now."

"Ah, do I have to? Just kidding, I want off these machines please!"

So, she took him off the machines, which made him wheeze. I immediately helped him into his clothes, though it was very disturbing. Then she hooked him back up. He was once again smiling. Our parents signed the papers and we started going to the van. I pushed his wheelchair.

"So, Mom, how's Jefferson and Destiny?" asked Jake, always so concerned about his family.

"They're taking it okay," replied my mother.

"Dad, Mom, what about y'all?"

Mom didn't reply and my dad mumbled something

that I couldn't understand.

Then Jake looked up into my eyes. I know he wanted to ask me the same question, but I couldn't let him see me be the way that I am; a coward. So I said, "Hey Peter Pan, who are you going to ask to the prom? Wendy?"

He blushed and replied, "I'm gonna take Frankie."

"I wonder, what do you see in that girl?" and we got Jake in the van. Then the rest of us got in there after we put the wheelchair in the back of the van.

"For starters, she's so beautiful!" he exclaimed.

Beautiful? No, she is not beautiful. Daffy is the one who's beautiful, but as most people say, 'What's one man's trash is another man's treasure.'

As he saw my expression, he said, "I know, she's not the most beautiful girl on the outside, but on the inside, she's like hitting a homerun out of the park! That's what really makes me overwhelmed when I see her. I don't know how to explain it, but I know she's meant for me. You know?" and he flashed me his movie star smile.

"I guess," I replied.

"Like you are meant for Daffy."

I blushed and asked, "You really think so?"

"I know so! You're such a fun sponge and she's so fun! You'll balance each other out." I stuck my tongue out at him.

"Jack, you know I'm messin', don't ya?"

"Yeah, I do."

"But really you two would be perfect," and he laid down on top of me.

"When did you become so good at love?"

"Pssh, I've always been good at the love game! You

just hadn't noticed 'cause your head is always stuck in an astronomy book."

I laughed and said, "Sure."

Then I thought to myself, do I really know Jake? If I didn't notice him being a so-called romantic, then what else do I not know about Jake? What if I don't know him at all? No, I won't focus on that right now.

Chapter Six
Failing as Captain

The next day I went to school. I didn't want to leave Jake, but I couldn't stay home. So, there was I standing in front of the school, alone and bitter. I didn't have many friends, but I sure did have lots of enemies, I realised that that day. I never had so much swirlys in my life! I guess my brother always got in the way of the so-called cool kids trying torturing me. Sure, I got picked on now and then, but never like this. Also, suspenders are apparently not cool. No lie, they called me 'Suspender Boy' and they laughed like it was funny. I beg to differ that treatment. It is not fun to be made fun of.

Well, after school, was baseball practice. I don't think it's going to go well. I am so terrified that I will mess up. It was like a million knots throughout my body.

"Well, we are going to start some um drills," I announced nervously.

"What kind, captain?" Lin sneered.

"Be nice, Brudder," Hug Man rebuked.

"How about we, uh, do a small scrimmage?"

"Okay," the team said in unison.

"Um, we won't have any outfielders, so no hard batting. Hug Man, Lin, Rose, Frances, Weird Frankie, and Jay is on team Blue. The rest is with me on team Red. Team Blue is up to bat."

So, we all got ready to play. Randy was on first base, Daffy was on second, Doll was short stop, Geo was third, Snickers was the catcher, and I was the pitcher. It sounded great, except for my position. I do NOT like pitching.

I threw my first ball and Hug Man got a homerun. Great, the first pitch of the game and it became a homerun. The next up to bat is Lin. This will be hard. He's hard to strike out. I threw the ball and he too, got a homerun. I realised something now, they are all going to Doll. She is no short stop. So, I switched her with Geo. The next one is Weird Frankie. I better strike him out. Snickers gives me the sign to throw a curve ball. I can throw a curve ball. It's simple, right? Well, I tried and I failed. I do not know what I threw. All I know was that it was the most horrible pitch in the record of horrible pitches. Also, Weird Frankie, the worst player on the team, got a homerun.

I looked behind me when the ball went flying and as far as I could tell, the usual outfielders were not good in the infield. I sighed and slapped my head, knowing this was a bad set up. Then we switched sides.

Now, it's Rose on first base, Weird Frankie on second, Lin on short stop, Jay on third base, Frances as catcher, and Hug Man as pitcher. Maybe this will go better, I hope.

Daffy is up to bat and Hug Man gives her a fast ball. Strike one. Another fast ball and she hits a Popfly toward

Rose. Rose wasn't able to catch it, so Weird Frankie ran off to get it at the same time as Rose. They ran into each other, causing Daffy to get a homerun. I slapped my head, acknowledging this was a bad setup also. Doll was up next and once again, Hug Man threw a fast ball. Can he throw anything else? Doll hit a homerun. Snickers was up next and once again another fast ball and once again a home run. I realised right then and there, there was no pitcher on their team. This was going to be a horrible game.

Like my prediction, it was a horrible game. We tied up for everyone got a homerun, even I got a homerun. After that, I decided to let everyone go home. Then I went home.

I angrily walked into the house and into my room, slamming my door for the joy of the noise it brought along with it. I climbed into my bed, hiding my face into my pillow. Then I did what I always do when I'm mad; hum as loud as I can.

A knock soon came to the door. "Go away!" I shouted.

"Too late, I'm already in here," said Jake.

"Get out."

"What's the matter?"

"Nothin's the matter."

"Really? You're humming like an angry hummingbird and you never say 'nothin's'."

I looked into his eyes and mumbled, "I had a bad day."

He sat beside and impersonated Mom's voice, "What's the matter, sweetie?"

"Really? Mom's voice?"

"Well, of course! It gets me in the therapist mood. Now, tell me, what went wrong today?"

"Everything!" I ranted and threw up my arms. "Everybody made fun of me at school today and don't get me started on baseball practice!"

Then he started laughing his hearty laugh. After he laughed for a good five minutes, he said, "Whew! That was funny!"

"What's so funny? That I got laughed at?"

"Oh no! Not at all!"

"Then what is it?"

"I forgot to tell you who's good at each position."

Then I threw my pillow at him and shouted, "Why didn't you tell me before?"

"I don't know. I guess I forgot. C'mon, let's go outside and talk baseball."

Chapter Seven
"Talking Baseball"

Once we were outside on the back porch, his mouth began to fly. Frankie is a catcher and only a catcher. She is the best batter, except for Jake, of course. Randy is on first base, but he can also pitch. He CANNOT be in the outfield. Daffy is on second base and can be anywhere in the outfield. Lin is short stop and any infielder. Jay just stays on third base. Geo is only an outfielder. Doll can be in left field and first base. And he talked on and on and on. Finally he got on the topic of me.

"So, how did you do?" he asked.

"Okay," I shrugged.

"Okay? You're the twin of the great Jake and you did okay?" He was so offended.

"I can't pitch so good."

"'Pitching is always a weird, difficult thing'."

"Who said that?"

"J.J. Abrams, the director of 'Armageddon'. The point is, is that it takes practice to become a good pitcher and you never pitched before. So, c'mon, let's practice."

"No, you are not playing baseball!"

"I ain't! Golly, I was gonna teach ya with words like I always do. Now, go get a ball and a mitt and let's pitch!" I quickly ran into my room and came back outside with some balls and mitt.

"Now," said Jake, "in order to be a good pitcher, you need accuracy. So, throw the ball in between that red circle on the fence."

I looked at the way he pointed his finger. That red circle? It's so tiny! How in the world can you throw a ball in between that circle?

"That circle?" I exclaimed, as I pointed at the same circle.

"Yes, that circle. What? You chicken?"

"Pssh! No, of course not!"

"Well then, throw the ball, but don't worry about how fast it is, just the accuracy."

Just the accuracy, got it! I wound up my ball as I saw my brother have done and threw. It was a little close to the circle.

"That's okay for the first try. Just go a little higher," he said.

A little higher, got it! I wound my arm up again and it went almost over the fence. "Go a little lower."

Okay. Maybe I got it this time? Nope, I threw a grounder. How does he do it? When you're out in the outfield, all you have to do is throw it to a person far away, not that close. Maybe that's my problem; I'm used to throwing from the outfield.

I got upset and like a middle school baseball player, I threw my glove onto the ground and stomped on it.

That was when my brother came to the rescue. He

put his hand on my shoulder and said, "It's okay, you're used to the outfield. That's what messing you up. You are accurate, the first pitch was a strike."

"Then what's with the circle?"

"That's because I finally calculated the most accurate spot to match Frankie's glove. See? I can say fancy words too."

I laughed. Silly Jake, always being goofy. "I can perceive that you can say such extravagant words. Do you acknowledge that I can say more elaborate words?"

"Duh! You're a nerd, nerd. So, let's get back to pitching."

I did, but only once did I make it in between the circle. It is true, I am meant for the outfield. Really, put me any position in the outfield. I don't want to pitch anymore.

Chapter Eight
First Game with Me as Captain

We were in the dugout, waiting for the blues to tell us who's going to start on offence and who's going to start on defence. I was so nervous; my breakfast was almost all over the ground. I was pacing back and forth as my team stared at me. As I can tell from their faces, they also was nervous. I knew I needed to say some inspirational speech as Jake always did, but I have never been good at giving speeches, unless I am talking about something like the molecular structure of an atom. But, other than that, I cannot get one word out of my mouth. But, they are worried, and with that negative mindset they will not do a good job. So, here it goes.

"Hey um, we need to not be so worried. Like I have read from somewhere, 'Think like a proton and stay positive'," I announced.

They looked at me with a baffling look.

I sighed and slapped my head. I forgot, I need to speak baseball, not science.

"'Never let the fear of striking out get in your way.' Babe Ruth. Don't be afraid, we can do this, with or without Jake. Now, let's get that trophy!"

We started out at defence. The usual starters was there, except for Hug Man. He took my place and I was pitching. I knew this game was not going to go well.

We were up against the Tigers. The first one came and as I can see from his face, he was delighted. I knew he had heard of my brother's absence due to cancer. But, that delight that marks his face should not lie thereupon. Anger arose to my burning, red cheeks. I shall defeat this team. I wound up my arm and gave him a fast ball. But, he knocked it to the outfield, strait towards Hug Man. I crossed my fingers, hoping that he would catch it. But, he didn't. He ran and got the ball and threw it to second, but the Tiger got there first.

The next Tiger came up. I gave him a curve ball and he hit towards Randy. Randy caught it and threw the Tiger out.

The third one came up, ready to hit it out of the park. I threw him a knuckle ball, but it turned out to be a ball. I threw him a sinker, but once again it was a ball. Then I gave him a shuuto ball and I walked him. Now, there is one Tiger on second base and another on first. What else can I screw up? Hey, why don't I throw a screwball?

The next one came up and I threw screwball. He hit it all the way to the end of the fence, causing two people to go Home and the last on third. I was frustrated by then. How can this be so hard? Can't they just let me strike them all out? I decided to never throw screwballs ever again.

The next Tiger was a small girl of probably fourteen years of age. I'm guessing they thought since I can't pitch very good to bring in their worst player. Well, I threw another fastball and she swung and missed. Strike two. Strike three. Out.

Next one up was another scrawny girl. I threw her a slurve ball. She hit it towards Lin. He caught it, causing her to go out.

We changed sides and we did much better at offence. We got four runs during that one inning. We changed back again and I decided to put Randy as pitcher, Hug Man on first base, and I was back in the outfield. I was happy with this arrangement… until they got eight runs in that one inning. Where did this all go wrong? I don't understand!

Well, the game ended and we lost. It was 5-18. I finally figured out our problem once the game was done. It was Hug Man. He cannot be put at first base. I totally forgot.

Well, they all sat around me, waiting for their captain to give them an encouraging speech. How can I do that? We all sucked out there. But, I must 'Think like a proton and be positive'. This time, I'm going to talk baseball, for the first time.

"Well, we all know that we didn't knock it out of the park this time," I said. See what I did there? Baseball talk. "But we must do what William Hickson said, 'If at first you don't succeed, try, try again.' So, we must keep trying to win. Just don't give up. Now, everybody run a lap around the field and then go home"

So, that was what we did. I was so disappointed in myself. I felt as if I brought the team down. I didn't even tell my brother what happened at the game, but he did find out from Randy.

Chapter Eight
Asking Someone Out for Prom

Games went by and we have significantly improved, though we lost about five of our games. And now everyone at my school is babbling about prom. Blah! Prom! I don't hate prom, just that it can be so annoying. The man has to buy the little flower thing, whatever it is, rent out an elaborate tux, nervously take her out onto the dance floor, and try to dance with elegance. But before all of this, they have to ASK the girl out. I cannot even ask a girl to borrow a pencil! How does someone expect me to ask a girl out on a date, not to mention my first date? I rather stay home in my sweats and watch the science channel. But, my brother says this is an amazing opportunity to ask Daffy out. I know he's right, but I am too scared to do so.

The one person that's way too excited for prom is Jake. He can't wait to swing Frankie all over the dance floor. He wants to ask her out, he wants to buy the flower thing, and everything else that pertains to prom. He really baffles me sometimes. He is not concerned about how weak he has gotten, but about his hair. He has lost every bit of his hair now since he has started chemo. He has tried on so many wigs, that I have lost count.

It was a usual Saturday. I got up in my cool, limited edition monster onesie. I ran downstairs and got down my favourite cereal, Count Chocula, and made myself a bowl of it. I got on the couch and put on my favourite cartoon, Toonsylvania. I know I am a scientist, but I am watching a kid's cartoon in a kid's set of PJ's eating a kid's cereal. But hey, I am not perfect. So, there I was, having the time of my life, when my brother came up and messed it up, as usual.

"Hey, when are you going to ask Daffy to prom?" asked Jake.

"Later, now can you leave so I can watch my cartoon? Seriously, can't a scientist be left in peace?" I angrily asked.

"Oh, I thought you would've said NOW, because she should be here, in like, a minute."

"She can't see me like this! How dare you forget my Saturday routine! You know I sleep in and do odd things on Saturdays. This is my day to be weird!"

"No, you're always weird."

"You know what I mean!"

A ding dong flourished throughout the house. I shrieked and hid behind the couch. Jake opened the door and cried, "Hey Daffy! How are you?"

"I'm good, how have you been?" she replied.

"Okay, still living. Glad for it. Wanna come in? Oh, Jack is behind the couch."

Darn it, brother! He needs to keep his mouth shut sometimes. No, like most of the time. This is going to ruin me! I popped out from behind the couch and said nervously, "Hey."

"Hey, Jack! You're wearing a funny onesie!" she laughed.

Well, there goes my chance. My elaborate chance of the most beautiful night of my life. Whoopie, thank you Jake Mark Davidson. You just ruined my life.

"Yeah," I said, looking at my shoes.

"Why so down? I have one just like it! I be-dazzled it to look more girly!" she giggled.

I brightened as fast as I went down. "Really? Where did you get?"

"I had it specially made!" we said at the same time. Then we blushed and looked away.

"Wow!" Jake said, surprised. "Well, I'll leave you two weird lovebirds do you. I'm gonna go to my room."

"Yeah, go have fun," I said, and it sounded like I was not even there.

"So..." she began.

"So..." I said.

"Why did your brother call for me to come here?"

"I don't really know, but I perceive it to be because of the prom."

"What do you mean?"

"I..."

"You like me?" she squealed so loudly, I was pretty sure my ears were about to burst. "Because I totally like you! You are so handsome! Okay, pick me up at seven!" Then she kissed my cheek and skipped out of the door.

Wow, I cannot believe this. Pretty Daffy likes me! She thinks I'm handsome! Wow, I need to take this in slowly.

"EHHHHHHHHHHH!" Jake squealed from behind. "That was so awesome!"

"Jake, were you spying on me?" I asked suspiciously.

"Maybe... yes, I was spying on you. But, look brother, you are going on your first date and then off to marriage!"

"Marriage?! No, one step at a time."

"Then you'll have a baby and call him Jake, after me. It'll be like a replacement of me."

A replacement of him? No, I don't need no replacements! I can't believe he said that to my face!

But, I was not going to get mad now. No, I'm going to change the subject. "Well, let's go talk to Frankie."

"No!" he shouted. "I can't do that! No, she won't want to date me."

"Why not? Y'all have been close friends since we were babies."

"I can't let her see me this way."

Was that a tear? Yes, that was a tear. I need to comfort him somehow. So, I went to him and hugged him, though it was so uncomfortable.

"Look, Peter Pan, she won't mind. This might be your last chance to take Frankie out on a date."

"What if she does, Jack? Then I'll have just missed out on a romantic night with my love."

I put his head up and looked him into his tear-filled eyes. "Trust me, she won't mind any of it. You will have your night."

As he is, he brightened up, dancing stars in his eyes. "Okay, let's go!"

"Right now?"

"Yes, right now."

"What about my TV show?"

"It's probably a re-run anyway. Let's go, but before that, go get out of that weird onesie."

"It's not weird, just unique."

"Like I said, it's weird."

"Unique!"

"Just go!"

So, I went upstairs and got my lime green sweatpants, my t-shirt that has a laser kitten on, my colourful suspenders, and my favourite hat upon my head. Then we got in the car and I drove to Frankie's house. We were soon upon her doorsteps.

"No, I can't do this!" Jake protested.

"Just push the doorbell," I commanded.

"No, I can't!"

"Just push it!"

Then we started to argue as siblings do. Finally, I grabbed his finger and pushed the doorbell with it. In just a few seconds, Frankie appeared, causing us to stop.

"Heyyyyyy," said Jake as he put his elbow on the door. I slapped my head. What an idiot thing to do!

"Hey Jake, how are you?" Frankie asked. Is she blushing? She's blushing! Yes, he's going to get his date!

"Okay, still living. Well, I was wondering, would you like to go to prom with me?"

"You want to go with ME?!"

"Well, of course; I've had a crush on you since third grade."

"Well then, yes! Yes, I'll go with you!"

"Okay, I'll pick you up around seven."
"Around seven, got it!"
"See you then!"
"See ya!"

Then the door was shut. Then Jake started whooping like a Native American. Then he started running up and down the streets.

"Jake, don't run! That's not good for you!" I shouted.

Then my brother collapsed in the middle of the road. Somebody honked their horn, but of course, Jake could not hear it. I ran out into the road and shielded my brother with my body before it hit him. A crash was heard and glass shattered. Then darkness covered my eyes.

Chapter Nine
Who are You?

I woke up in a hospital bed and the sound of beeping came flooding to my ears, and pain shot throughout my body. I looked around my room, expecting to see my family, but they were not there. Then I saw a person that I have never seen before. Who is he?

"Beg my pardon, but I believe you are in the wrong room," I said to the boy.

"No, you are," he said.

Now that was creepy! What in the world is he talking about? "Excuse me?"

"Oh sorry, Jack, I just wanted to sound creepy for a second. How is your brother?"

"How do you know my name?"

"I guess you don't pay attention to your own surroundings. I am Peter, Jake's chemo buddy."

Peter? Oh, yes! Peter! He's Jake's chemo buddy. There's this thing at the hospital for teenagers thirteen to seventeen to take chemo in the same room. They hang out for an hour and talk to each other. The doctors says it calms them, allowing their bodies to take in the chemo better.

"Oh yes, I forgot! Jake is doing fine," I said.

"Great!" he exclaimed. "But, my concern is more on you."

"Me? Why me?"

"How are you taking it?"

"Taking what?"

"How your brother, twin, best friend, protector, etc. is going to die?"

"I... I... I..." I stammered over and over. I had no words to express how deeply affected I was. I felt like someone was taking a knife to my heart and kept twisting it, though they know I am already dead inside.

"I know you are hurting. I can see it in your eyes." And he sat close to me. "But, did you know that you can be with him forever?"

"What do you mean?" I really want to know if I could be with him forever.

"There is a place called Heaven, and a place called Hell. And one day, you will go to either one of them."

"Uh huh, tell me more."

"Heaven is a place full of gold and Hell is full of fire. If you die in sin, you will go to Hell."

"What do you mean?"

"I guess I have to go to the beginning. When humans was first made by God, God made Adam and Eve. God placed them in a garden and told them they can eat of every tree, but of the Tree of the Knowledge of Good and Evil."

"Why?"

"Because if they did, then they would die spiritually.

This meant they would be separated from God by sin. Well, they did, causing all of humankind to be filled with sin. Since God loves us, He decided to send His Son, Jesus, to pay for all of our sins, so we can go to Heaven and never be separated from Him."

"How did He pay?"

"Since the payment of sin is death, He died on the cross, taking sin upon Himself. Then He was buried and rose again three days later, conquering death. All we have to do is believe He did this. Like it says in John 3:16, 'For God so loved the world that he gave his only begotton Son that whosoever believeth in him should not perish, but hath everlasting life.' You see, y'all can be together forever. Didn't Jake mention this to you?"

"No, he hasn't."

Then my family, except for Jake, came into the room.

"Think about it, Jack. Mr. and Mrs. Davidson." Then he was gone.

How can this be true? It doesn't make since! I need to talk to Jake, but first, I need to get out this hospital. I knew my brother was going to put me in here someday. Ha, ha, funny! Right?

Chapter Ten
Talking to Jake About This

I was released the day afterward. It was a thing that nobody could explain, not even a scientist. A miracle? I think that's what it's called. I did not have any broken bones, just a few scratches. The doctor could not even explain it to me. Jake also came out the next day unharmed. I was so glad to see him come out in a wheelchair beside me.

We were finally at the house and our parents confined us to the couch, lest we do any more dangerous shenanigans. I decided that this would be the perfect opportunity to talk to him about Heaven and Hell.

"Jake, could I talk to you about Peter?" I asked out of the blue.

"What about him?" he replied.

"He came into my room yesterday and he was talking about Heaven and Hell."

"What about it?"

"How to get to Heaven. He said that you already accepted this idea. Is this true?"

"For starters, it's real, not an idea. And yes, I did

accept Jesus into my heart."

"I don't understand."

"Uh, I have to explain this in your language. Let's think of how this world was made. The world, by your perspective, was made by the Big Bang. But think of how wonderfully a lot of things are made, like how the air is: if there is too much, I think it is carbon, in the air, then we would have carbon monoxide, causing no life on this planet called Earth. This gives a sign of a Creator. Then there's something wrong with evolution. How can a fossilised dinosaur be million years old when Earth is only about six thousand years old? And how can evolution be accurate when, for example, if we came from monkeys, the hard process of them evolving into us would cause a deficiency in their survival? They would be all deformed before they became humans, but they aren't changing now, and are perfectly formed. This too shows a sign of a Creator."

"Okay, then why make us, if He did?"

"For His pleasure."

"That is not logical when He owns the universe."

"Look, am I pleasurable to you?"

"Yes."

"Then it is like that for God. Yes, He has His Son and the Holy Spirit, but I bet He got lonely talking to Himself. So, He made the angels, but they were made to obey."

"That would have sufficed me."

"Well, think about this. Would you rather have a robot as a friend who is made to love and adore you, or someone who chose to love you?"

"Someone who chose to love me."

"So, when we disobeyed Him, He was upset. We longer could be His friends forever. So, He chose to send His Son to die for our sins. Now, all you have to do is believe and you would be with me forever."

"Oh."

All I have to do is believe? Wow, that's so easy! How can it be so easy? It's just way too easy for such a glamorous reward.

A silence passed us, until I asked, "Why have you never shared this with me before?"

"Because you are too much of a scientist to believe something that you cannot see. I'm sorry, I should have mentioned it before."

"No, you have no need to apologise."

"Good, now let's finish this weird cartoon that you love."

But, I didn't want to finish the cartoon. I was too baffled with this this Heaven and Hell thing that I could not even hear the joyful laughter of the mad scientist.

Chapter Eleven
Shopping for a Tux!

A tux? A tux?! A TUX?! Why, oh, why a tux? Why not just a polo shirt and slacks? Please? Pretty please? But, no, it has to be a tux. And the flower thing. And the dancing, with a dance that has no art or grace. No, I cannot dance with elegance, even though I try. It is all in vain. Blah! Prom!

Well, Jake has to find the perfect tux. So, he has made a map of all the places he wants to go and the time it will take him to go to all twenty stores. It looks like a five year old trying to draw a professor-levelled chart with a crayon. I am not lying, but my twin did use a crayon on his chart.

So, we head out, with me regretting every mile. I do not like shopping, whether it is for the groceries or for a pair of shoes. I will forever hate shopping. Every place we went to, he made me try on at least one tux. They all looked the same to me, but Jake said they were different. I guess I'm blind to fashion.

It was like the fifty millionth store we went to when I found something interesting. The tux was completely covered in the solar system! I know I don't like tuxedos, but this one is actually pretty awesome. So, I took it from off the rack and headed to the dressing room. I put it on and stood in front of the mirror. I never realised this before, but I am actually pretty good looking! No, I am what girls would call the bomb diggidity! Actually, I am not that good looking, but still pretty handsome.

"Jack, you found something?" Jake called.

"Yeah!" I shouted.

"Then show me."

I came out and he laughed, as I knew he would. "You look like a nerd!" he laughed.

"I think I look rather smashing," I said, in a horrible fake British accent.

"You look rather nerdy!" he mocked. "Well, I like it. Did you find something?"

"No, not yet. But I have an idea." And he showed me a tux with baseballs all over. Of course, it would have baseballs all over.

"Well, try it on, Jake."

"But, don't it look weird?"

"I am wearing a tuxedo with the solar system all over. There is nothing weirder than that!"

"How 'bout that?" and he pointed to a tuxedo with lights all over.

"I stand corrected. Just try it on, it matches your demeanour."

He put it on and we stood in front of the mirror. There we are! Too completely different and, yet completely the same set of twins. I felt as if we were whole right there like I haven't felt in this past two months. We completed each other. Just us two, Jake and Jack. I will never forget that feeling.

"So, you think we should buy them?" asked Jake, bringing me back to reality.

"Buy them?" I asked, surprised. "I thought we were going to rent them out."

"Nah, I want to wear this at my funeral, same as you wear yours."

"Could you stop mentioning your funeral?" I was really angry at that moment.

"I'm sorry, I thought you were the only one I could talk to about it, but I guess I'm wrong. I have nobody."

"What are you talking about?" I cried out and touched his shoulder. "I'm always here for you."

He pushed me away and said, "Really? You don't act like it."

"What? I am your twin and you are accusing me of being forgetful of you?"

"Yes, I feel like I can't talk about me having cancer or dy…"

"No! Don't say it! I can't bear it any longer!" I got onto my knees and wept like I haven't done in a long time.

I can see my brother's eyes and they softened. Jake has always been the comforter and I could feel his comfort coming close to me. I know, I sound ludicrous.

"No!" I shouted. "No words, not even yours can comfort me. I have gone too far for words to comfort me. Just let me be!"

"Jack," my brother said. Oh, his voice sounded as if he was a sweet, heavenly angel. "I know words cannot comfort you, but just hear me out. There is nothing, no, not nothing that can separate us. Not even death is going to take me away from you. I know that was what you are afraid of, but I am here. My memory will always be lodged into that big brain of yours."

I couldn't help myself. I grabbed onto his tux and laid my head upon his bosom. There I cried. I know I will always remember him, but I want him to always be with me until the day I die.

Chapter Twelve
Prom

This is the day. The day that Jake has been looking forward to, but I have been dreading. I seriously want to puke right now. It is prom! Blah!

We started getting ready at five in the evening. I got done five minutes later. But, Jake disapproved of my appearance. He grabbed me and yanked me into his room. There he combed my hair. Apparently, we don't wear caps at prom. You think that since I am a nerd, I wouldn't want to wear a cap. But, it's so much easier than trying to tackle my mop. After he was done yanking at my hair, he did other things to me like spray some reeking cologne. I protested at everything he did, but since he insisted, I allowed him to make me over. After he was done with me, it hit six thirty. We were going to be late! Jake quickly yanked on his tux and sprayed the same nasty cologne on himself. I mean it, I can still smell that cologne to this day.

We soon came to Daffy's house. I nervously knocked on the door. She came out and what a beauty! She wore a beautiful solar eclipse dress. It was so short that I could see her legs and chest. Control yourself, Jack, control yourself.

I held out the flower thing and she squealed like she did last time. I'm not even in the noisy prom and you already broke my eardrums, woman!

"Oh Jack, it's so beautiful! It matches us!" she squealed and then jumped on top of me. Then she took a picture of us, without me realising it. "That's a keeper! Let's go get our groove on!"

"Okay!" I cried and put her in the van.

All the way to Frankie's house, she joked around. I never laughed like that in all my life! I thought I was going to die of laughter! That's what my younger siblings could have said to their grandkids. Oh, my brother Jack died of laughter when he was going to the prom and my brother Jake... I'm not going to think of his cancer tonight, but have fun, as I haven't had in a long time.

When we arrived at Frankie's house, Jake got out of the car. I followed soon thereafter, though he told me not to. I heard and saw everything.

Jake knocked on the door and Frankie came out. Her dress matched his, but that was not the only thing. She shaved her head completely bald! That is sheer kindness.

Jake put on the flower thing on her wrist and said, awe stricken, "Frankie, you look beautiful!"

"Really? Even though I am fat and bald?" she replied.

"I'm bald and I'm still attractive. Also, I don't care about your weight. You are beautiful inside and out. Why did you shave your hair?"

"For you, Jake. Remember, we're the great dynamic

duo. We stick together like glue. Also, I love you."

"I love you, too." I can hear the chock in his voice.

I can hear it, the bittersweet knowing that Frankie is his, at least for tonight. They have always stuck like glue since they were sweet, innocent babies. Now, this will be the last time.

They started to come to the car, and I hopped right in beside Daffy before they even noticed my spying. Off to the prom! Blah!

We soon arrived and the noise of music and shouting blasted all through the school. I led Daffy inside and we found a table. I needed to get used to this loud music before going onto the dance floor. But, Daffy didn't mind. She just kept on joking around, making me laugh. But, Jake went immediately onto the dance floor, not caring at all about his critical condition. I had a deep desire to take him home for his safety, but he was having so much fun. I just didn't dare to do such a thing. Well, by the doctor's predictions, he only has a few weeks left. So, I will not bother him.

Finally, I got used to the ruckus. I grabbed Daffy by the hand and led her to the dance floor. We did the cha-cha, swing, the Charleston, the Carlton, and whatever weird thing I came up with. It was so much fun! I didn't want it to end.

Well, the principal got up onto the stage and made the announcement that it was time to crown the prom king and queen. Everybody huddled around, hoping that it would be them. Well, that is, except for me. I hate being in the spotlight.

"The prom queen is..." the principal announced.

Drum roll. "Frances Daffodil!" And Frankie went up there and they put the crown upon her bare head. "And the prom king is…" Another drum roll. "Jake Davidson!" He too got up there and they put a crown upon his bare head. "Your prom king and queen! Now, for the spotlight dance!"

Music started to play, but then Jake stopped it. He whispered something into the DJ's ears. Then another song started to play. It was "Unchained Melody" by the Righteous Brothers. It was so perfect! The spotlight upon their crowned heads as he swung her around the floor. I can see tears flow from his eyes as her head rested upon his chest. They were alone for that single moment. Just everything was silent, but that one moment. "I need your love," sung throughout their bodies as they meant every step. They do need each other.

The music stopped playing and everybody cheered. I never found out who gave him that moment, but I thank you, whoever you may be, for doing that for my brother. It means a lot to me to know that you cared so much for him.

Chapter Thirteen
The Big Game

We made it! We are now in the championships! We are going up against the Bears. I am so nervous and excited all at the same time. I want to throw up, but then again I want to fly. Everybody in the dugout can see that, including my brother. He's going to pitch the first pitch of the game. I can't wait to see him bring the heat! Oh no, throw up!

Yeah, I threw up all over the dugout.

"Jack, calm down! Sit over here with me," Jake said.

"I can't, I can't sit down or calm down," I said and then threw up again.

"Sit!" Lin growled and forced me to sit. But, I threw up on him too. "Gross! Somebody give him a bucket before he completely ruins the dugout!" Lin then took his shirt off and threw it in the trash. I'm glad it wasn't his uniform; then I would've been dead!

Well, Hug Man did give me a bucket, but I didn't need it any longer. We are now starting the game. Jake got up on the mound and he took off his breathing machine and his IV. A smile flooded his face. He hasn't been on the mound since he discovered he was dying. It was the same Bear that he almost struck out, but didn't because he died in the middle of the pitch. He wound up his arm and gave that Bear a fast ball up to one hundred. Strike one. Strike two.

Then he wound up for his famous right handed submarine pitch. A flood of memories came back to me. I wanted to scream out Jake's name like I did before, but I refrained myself. Strike three. He's out.

Jake put his machines back on and left the mound to me. Sweat poured out of my pores. I can feel the ball slipping in my hands. I want to win so badly. I want to give Jake his most deserved championship trophy. I want to win. I need to win... for Jake.

I wound up my arm and gave him a fast ball. Strike one. Now, I need to give pitches as accurate as this. I give him a slider. Strike two. Stop sweating, Jack! I give a curve ball. He hit it all the way to the outfield to Geo. Out.

I am so nervous! We are 5–8. We are losing by three runs! I can't believe this! Oh, that's not why I'm nervous. I am the one batting! All the bases are filled, and I'm the one to get them all home. I look at the pitcher and I realised it was the Bear that Jake struck out this game. I do not want to lose to him, of all the people in the world.

He throws me a curveball. Strike one. Then he throws me a slider. Strike two. Then I fouled a ball off. Now, here it goes. I swing and the ball flies. I ran as hard as I could. I need to win. The third baseman has the ball. I start running to second. Second now has the ball. Aww man! I'm in a pickle! We start going back and forth, until third baseman threw the ball over second. I took off! I ran to third and then towards home. Second throws to home. I slide and safe! We won!

I ran to Jake and shouted, "We won!"

Randy came up behind us and shoved the big trophy into his arms. Then the whole team came and picked Jake up, machines and all. Then we chanted Jake over and over again.

I remember his face. He was so happy, tears fell out of his eyes. I love seeing him happy.

Chapter Fourteen
Our Birthday

It was May 1st 1998, mine and Jake's seventeenth birthday. I am soooooo happy! Especially since I get to spend it with Jake. I got up at nine and ran to Jake's room.
"Hey, wake up!" I cried.
"What do you want?" he mumbled.
"C'mon, we're going to have fun today!"
"What kind of fun? Yours or mine?"
"Yours, I'm skipping school today!"
"Wow, mister bad boy, are you really?"
"Yeah! I already talked to Mom about it."
"Even though you look like you're gonna die?"
"Why do you say that?"
"You're nervously biting your nails because you know your perfect attendance record is going down the drain, again."
"So what? My brother is more important. Let's do all those things you've always wanted to do."
"Even sky diving?!"
"Maybe."
"That's gonna be so awesome! What are we waiting

for?!"

"My guess is Mom."

"Well, let's go downstairs and eat."

We flew downstairs to CHOCOLATE PANCAKES, my favourite! I ate those pancakes faster than I could say the longest word in the world. I will always enjoy chocolate pancakes.

"Where are we going first, Mom?" asked Jake with his mouth full of pancake. "Why don't you give him a riddle to figure it out?" my mother asked me.

I thought for a second and then figured out a good riddle. I have always liked riddles. They are fun to make and figure out. It's like a math problem with more creativity. Well, this is what I said, "A place where things go round, and things you eat turn your frown upside down."

"'A place where things round and things you eat turns your frown upside down'?" Jake repeated.

"Any guesses?"

"Man, you…" he started to turn green. "I'll be back," and he ran off. I can hear from the dining room, my brother losing the few bites he has already eaten. He soon came back. "As I was saying, man you make good riddles!"

I closed my nose and swatted the air as if it was a fly. My brother's breath stunk so bad; as bad as the skunk who sprayed me when I was twelve.

"I'm sorry, I didn't mean for that," my brother apologised.

"It's okay. Now, any guesses?"

"No, I can't think of anything."

"What's your favourite baseball team of all time?"

"The Texas Rangers."

I pulled out three tickets from my pocket and put them in Jake's hand.

"Oh my gosh!" Jake shouted. "We're going to a Texas Rangers game! This is so exciting! Wait, is this reserved sitting with all those benefits like meet the players?!"

I nodded my head and my mother and I closed our ears because that's when my brother screamed with excitement.

"I am so excited! I get to meet my idol, Scott Bailes! I can't wait! Let's go now!" and he started to run out the door.

"Um, Jake, you're still in your PJ's!" I shouted.

"That's right!" and he ran upstairs.

I smiled to myself. This is going to be the best day of Jake's life, I guarantee it! I planned the whole day to be packed with all the things Jake loves.

The first thing we did was go to the baseball game. There he caught a foul ball and got it signed by Scott Bailes and the whole team. The whole team loved him! I never saw anybody so adored by famous people before; nor have I seen famous people before, but you know what I mean. Every last one of them got a picture with Jake.

Next thing we did was go to the Baseball Hall of Fame. I did not plan this, but the baseball players paid for us to go. Oh, I forgot to tell you, we got the Cancer Dream Program, or whatever it's called, to pay for the baseball tickets. I guess they told the Rangers we were coming. Jake took a picture in front of the picture of Babe Ruth. I was even siked about that!

Then we went to my brother's favourite restaurant, Waffle House. I was very surprised, he was actually eating! He hasn't ate a bite in four days! But I was very glad that he did.

Now, it's six in the evening. We got back on the plane and we were able to get back home at seven. It was dark in the house. We came in and light shot through the air and surprise rang my ears. There was the whole team! I definitely did not plan this!

"Happy Birthday, baby!" Frankie said and put a pointy weird hat upon my brother's head.

"Oh, you guys!" my brother cried. There was literal tears flowing from his eyes.

"Well, let's get this party started!" Lin shouted

Well, music started and the party went wild! I never had so much fun in my life until that night! We danced, we sang, we played games, we had cake and ice cream. It was the best birthday of my life! Until... it wasn't.

Once the party was done, my brother fell to the ground. The doctors that were there to take care of him at night rushed him upstairs. My family and I followed. There they told us that they didn't think he was going to make it through the night. Every last one of us started to cry. My brother assured them to not be scared, but to brave for someday they might see him again. They didn't understand, but they went along with him. Then he asked them to all leave, except for me to stay.

"Come and hold my hand," my twin said to me.

I ran and grabbed his hand. He squeezed it, but it didn't hurt. I knew he was dying right then and there. I looked into his eyes and all I saw was death. It scared me worse than when I first heard of his cancer.

"Jack," his voice was going away, "please, don't be afraid. Things happen for a reason. I know you're scared, but be brave for me. Will ya?" Tears rolled down his fearful eyes.

"I don't know how, but I'll try," I sobbed.

"That's good." Now, he is choking for air, though he had a machine on. "Go into my first drawer and take the Bible out." I did as he said and gave it to him. "Promise me that you'll give this to your first child and read it every day.

"Also, promise me that you'll be the scientist that you always wanted to be and not a baseball boy."

"I promise."

"Now, Jack, I will always miss you, for you are the dearest person in the world to me."

"Me too."

His grasp released and beeping noises flowed through the air. His eyes closed and I never heard his voice again. The doctors rushed in and was able to revive him. But he is now in a coma. I stayed up for most of the night, talking to him like he was still with me. But, I didn't last through the night. When I woke up the next morning, he was gone. It seemed as if he waited for me to go to sleep, so then I would not see him die.

Chapter Fifteen
The Next Few Days

The next day was Jake's funeral and as I promised, I wore my solar system tux, though my mother protested against such bright colours for a funeral. But, I was able to persuade her by mentioning my promise. Jake was also put into his prom tuxedo.

It seemed as if I was living in a bad dream. Some strangers were putting my brother into the ground. He's not dead! He's not dead! I ran to my brother's casket and clung to it. I protested that my brother was not dead, but they didn't believe me! They told my father to take me away, but I didn't want to leave. If they were going to bury my brother, they were to bury me too. I told them so too. That made my mother upset and made my father mad. He firmly said to me to stop my foolishness. I immediately stopped and the funeral proceeded.

I wouldn't stop jittering. They were burying my twin alive! How cruel of them! I couldn't think straight throughout the whole funeral.

The days after the funeral was a blur to me. I went to school most of the day, and the rest I laid in my brother's bed. I convinced myself a long time ago that he wasn't dead. I barely passed the eleventh grade that year. My GPA definitely went down the drain.

In the summer, I joined a gang. I don't remember when, nor do I remember how I did so, but I did. I lost many friends that year, except for Daffy. I soon impregnated her a few months after my brother's death. That was when my father put down some ground rules. Firstly, I had to get married to her. I did on Christmas day. She soon gave birth to my firstborn, Jake Davidson.

My bad boy years did not end though. No, I did every possible bad thing you could imagine. All I wanted to do was to get rid of the memory of my brother. I soon dropped out of baseball because it only brought me pain. Then I dropped out of high school. Thinking I could get a job with my new found friend, I left my home, taking my wife and young child with me. We were soon on the streets, begging for food and searching for survival.

I was nineteen years old and I will never forget this day. We had been on the streets for one year now and we found ourselves in front of a church in Louisiana.

"Jack, we need to find some food for Jake. He's hungry and I no longer have milk to feed him. Please, go into that church and beg for food for us."

"But, Daffy, it's a church!" I protested.

"If Jake doesn't get any food, he will starve to death! Do you want our child to die?"

"No, I don't. Wait outside and I will come back for you."

I walked into the church and the first thing I saw was John 3:16 upon the wall. Yes, as I promised my brother, I have read the Bible, but not every day. I was so mad.

'For God so loved the world...' sprang out like a Jack in the Box. If he loved me, why did he let this happen? Why did he let Jake die? I was so infuriated I threw Jake's Bible at the cross that was in front of the stage.

"Why?" I shouted at the top of my lungs. "Why did you take away my brother? Why bring poverty to me?" I did not realise this, but I was crying. I remembered something that my brother once said before he died, 'Things happen for a reason.' What is this reason? Why me?

I sat there crying for a good ten minutes. Suddenly, I decided I don't want to live like this anymore. I wanted the life that Jake deserved to live. How am I to acquire this life? I remembered in the Bible how so many people had happy, beautiful lives after giving their hearts to the Lord. I wanted that life, happy and beautiful. Also, I wanted to see Jake again. So, that day I gave my heart to the Lord. It was the happiest day of my life and from then on my life was completely changed around.

Chapter Sixteen
My Last Game

It is now May 2nd 2018, the anniversary of my brother's death. I am now 36 and I play for the Texas Rangers, though my brother insisted me to be a scientist and not a baseball boy. But, I didn't obey his requests. No, I thought I would be much happier fulfilling my brother's dreams through me.

We are playing a game today, and when I mean we, I mean my old team and others. Well, the girls were not there, of course. We are playing at my old high school, due to the MLB allowing me to pick the place since it was going to be my last game. Oh, I forgot to tell you, I am world famous.

We ran out onto the field and there I can see my family. There was my mother and father watching me. There was Daffy and my seven children, except for my eldest. He's playing on the team with me for the first time. Then there is Destiny and her husband and her two kids. Then there is Jefferson and his wife, Frankie, and their kid. If you are wondering, yes, it is the same Frankie that once loved Jake. She said that she loved my family too much to give it up. But since I was a bad boy then and I reminded her too much of Jake, she gave up on trying me out. So, she tried Jefferson out and it is true, they worked out perfectly. They love each other very much.

We got into the dugout to go over the game plan with couch, but I was not focused. I can't stop my thoughts from turning to my dearest brother, Jake. Randy saw I couldn't pay attention, so he put his hand upon my shoulder.

Then he whispered into my ear, "I know, I miss him as well." I smiled back at him.

We came back out and now I am going to pitch. But, first they are letting me give a speech.

"Hello ladies and gentlemen!" I announced. "Welcome to the championship game! I am so honoured to be here. My family has always asked me why I chose to become a baseball player. And this is what I always tell them: when I was a boy I wanted to be a scientist. I did not really care for baseball, but my twin did. He lived and breathed baseball. But, when he got cancer one year, he could no longer play. He died nineteen years ago today. I went into total chaos. But, when I turned nineteen, I found myself and God. Right there, I also decided to do something with my life worthwhile. Yes, I could have been a scientist and a great one too, but that was not what I decided. I decided to fulfil my brother's dreams that day. But, my time of baseball is at its end. So, tonight after this game, I am to retire. And by my request, the Texas Rangers are allowing my firstborn to play with us tonight, though it is the last game of the season. But, he will be back next year as my replacement. I am proud of you my son. Now, who's ready to play some ball?"

The crowd cheered.

"That's what I thought so. Let's play ball!"

So, I got up to plate. We went up against the Red Sox. I wound up my arm and gave that Red Sox a fast ball of one hundred miles per hour. Strike one. Then I gave him a curveball. Strike two. Strike three. Out. I stroke the next two players out.

It went by like this: I stroke them out and they stroke us out. It was soon 5–5. It seemed like we were getting nowhere! Like at my last game of my high school years, I was the one to save this game. The bases were filled and I was up to bat. I was so nervous! I sweated from head to toe! I can tell that this was the Bear that Jake struck out before he died. I cannot let this man strike me out! He first gave me a fast ball and I swung too early. I can hear from the dugout Geo screaming to me to calm down. Then the once Bear gave me a curveball. Once again, I stroke out because I swung too early. Next ball he gave me, I hit that ball so hard it went out of the park.

I won that day. I was very happy that I could give Jake another trophy. Well, I forgot why I am telling you my story, but I do have something to say. No matter how bad it gets, look to God and let Him be the One to help you. God bless and have a nice day!

Acknowledgements

To my wonderful friend and saviour, God. I would like to thank Him for all that He has done for me and giving me the willingness to pursue this passion that He has put into me. Also, to my loving and caring brother, Jeffrey. Thank you for always being there for me even when I made you mad sometimes. You are a good person, Jeffrey.

CPSIA information can be obtained
at www.ICGtesting.com
Printed in the USA
BVHW081202210321
603030BV00007B/1411

9 781839 340598